Be here now
Trust your soul
Open your heart

Follow the wisdom
of your body

Everything
you need to know
is already
inside you

Soulful Business Journal

Grow your business with the energy
of the four seasons

Eos Koch

Contents:

YOUR
HEART
IS YOUR
GUIDING
STAR

Dear beautiful soul,

Honoring the cycles, growth, and reflections on where we are in our business for me has become a ritual.

As a way to grow my business, I am present with my own rhythm through my menstrual cycle, the cycle of the moon, the stars, and the seasons.

I take time during my days and weeks when I need to fill up my energy, so I can give, serve and show up from a place of fullness, service, and love. Each of these cycles offers me different connection points and is an invitation to drop deeper to be able to serve from a place of love and devotion.

It is the slowing down and taking on an outside perspective that is so precious, while the day-to-day work and inspired action taking is the heart pulse of our businesses, the reflections and intentions are the places where we create magic and direct the flow of energy.

Following an outside blueprint with all its promises never worked for me. The programs, coachings, and online courses that leave open space to follow and implement what is right for me were always the ones that worked for me and brought the most change and this is the way I work in everything I do.

In all my work, my intention is to openly share my experiences.

I show up in full presence and then it is your part to take the responsibility and make it right for you.

I trust in you. You are a powerful creator of reality. Own your power and allow transformation through love.

As a collective, our planet is in the phase of growth. We are pushed and held accountable to our own values of integrity and truth. What sometimes looks like chaos, is the letting go of something we thought we were and the elevation into deeper parts of who we are.

Your fear is your gift.
It is the invitation for collective change and transformation.

We do have the choice to take on our own self-responsibility and anchor in a new way of relating and being through our living embodiment.

This growth and this change we are in right now as the beautiful beings living on planet earth can feel so big, but we are not alone. We all in one way or the other meet the parts in ourselves that have the potential to transform and take new shape.

And through the transformation from fear to love inside of us, we create ripples in the world.

Ripples of compassion, deeper acceptance, truth, and pure love. So we can remember, who we are in our essence.

My intention for this journal and the questions is that you collect your learnings, reflect on your growth and consciously direct the energy of your life and business.

Creation is a dance of masculine and feminine energy.

Supporting the feminine way of expression and expansion while holding our work in a masculine container of structure.

To me, this journal is part of the container and structure a soulful business needs so we can do our work infused and birthed from an open and loving heart.

Take some time for yourself. Prepare a cozy place, light a candle, put on some music and make yourself a warm beverage.

Wishing you a beautiful deep dive and may you trust yourself.
With Love,
Eos

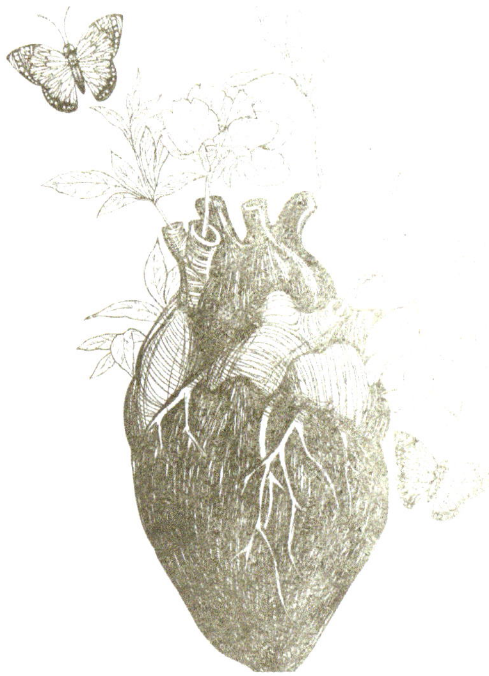

Committment *creates* momentum.

Your energy investment creates a magnetic field that attracts everything to you that you show up for in the invisible realms of thought and energy.

Action is your power of creation.

Make space in your heart, your mind, and your soul. Be intentional with the things you show up for in your life.

Vision and Intention

Winter is fire energy. Time to focus and go inward to gather your power. This is the season of introspection, to hibernate, and the perfect time of the year to put the seeds of your intentions into the soil to germinate.

Time to reflect and look back on the past year and its cycles. Setting a new intention for the year ahead and connecting deeply with your visions and desires. Winter starts with the day with the least light in the yearly cycle and from there builds up moving towards Spring where your desires, visions, and ideas will start to sprout.

Winter is the time to connect with your inner world.

I set my intentions for the year at the beginning of Winter. I connect first with where I am and what I desire. Letting go of outside expectations and getting clear on my path from where I am to where I want to be.

Take some uninterrupted time for yourself. Cuddle onto a comfy place, light a candle, put on some music, and make yourself a warm beverage. Reflect on the questions and shape your path for the coming year consciously.

Reflection on how far you have come

What are you most excited about in life right now?

Where were you last winter? What visions and intentions did you set for yourself?

Did you have a word for the year? What did this word teach you?

What gifts gave you this year?

Who have you become?

What was the hardest thing for you this year?

What did you learn from this year? What experiences did this create for you?

What kind of new behavior, change, and growth did this year bring you?

Where did you tell yourself things are not possible?

How can you take the power back and make things possible for you?

Where do you look outside for solutions instead of finding them inside of you?

Where and for what did you find innovative solutions this year?

What did you learn and want to anchor in for the future from these experiences?

How will you celebrate all the good things from this year?

I have a *grateful* heart for

Vision on where you want to go

What do you want more of in the coming year?

What do you want less of in the coming year?

Trust *yourself*

Who do you want to be and become during this year?

What do you want to do this year? What do you want to practice?

What physical possessions do you want to create for yourself? What do you desire to have?

What outside expectations do you need to let go to get there?

What needs to happen to call those intentions into your life and business?

What are the three most important intentions and desires you have for this year?

1.

On a scale from 1 to 10 how willing are you to invest yourself in making them a reality?

I hope it happens — I am willing to invest myself — I will do whatever it takes

2.

On a scale from 1 to 10 how willing are you to invest yourself in making them a reality?

I hope it happens — I am willing to invest myself — I will do whatever it takes

3.

On a scale from 1 to 10 how willing are you to invest yourself in making them a reality?

I hope it happens — I am willing to invest myself — I will do whatever it takes

How realistic feel they for you?

Which one is the most important to you and a priority this season? Usually the one with the highest rating.

The world needs you embodied in your *essence*

Why do you want to make this intention come true?

What will be the biggest obstacle? Where will you have the most resistance?

What is the worst that could happen if you commit and walk towards your intention?

What do you need to let go to get there?

How will you feel when you will reach our intention?

How can you make yourself feel this way on the path to your intention?

In which areas do you want to invite support?

What new things do you want to learn?

What is an adventure or experience you want to create for yourself this coming year?

How will you grow and expand your current comfort zone? Share three things that feel outside your comfort zone that would make you grow if you would do them.

1.

2.

3.

To what actions do you regularly commit? What do you want to practice?

In which way will you hold yourself accountable?

Map out the steps you need to take to get from where you are today, to where you want to be at the beginning of Spring!

WHERE I AM TODAY

WHERE I WANT TO BE

Trust your *journey*

When you feel out of alignment, what helps you to get back and motivated? Write a list with five ideas.

Anchor in your vision and intention

Choose a word for the year. You can go back and look through your answers and collect all the feeling words in your answers.
Allow your word to emerge intuitively. There is no right and wrong way to do this. The only important thing is that you feel it in your body.

Create a vision board for Winter.

Collect images that feel right for you and cut or print them out. Your soul knows what you desire. Allow yourself to be guided and choose the images that speak to you at the moment without analyzing them.

Your vision board:

To get a new outcome, we need to travel new roads.

Every physical action has its starting point in the unseen.

Everything starts as potential.

There are infinite possibilities right now in front of you that you could choose right at this moment.

We are used to making the choices that we made in the past over and over again because we already have the neurons in our mind connected in the way of least resistance.

Our mind is a net of electricity.

The paths well-traveled, are the paths that build our character and make us who we are.

We travel a certain route in our mind, that creates a certain outcome in our physical reality, and we take that route again and again.

The older we get, the more we have premade paths of thoughts in our mind and the more fixed we are getting in our thinking.

This premade path of electric charge in our mind is what makes us into who we are.
The pain we meet, the limitations we encounter, the good things we allow into our life. We do have set these experiences as electrical circuitry in our minds.

We can reroute this circuitry and make new connections.

When we stop defining ourselves from who we were in the past and start fully embodying the moment while letting ourselves be guided towards the life we desire to live.

This is inspired action.
Moving from the present moment.

Letting go of who you thought you are, so you can fully embody the version of you that you desire to be.

Bloom and Grow

Spring is air energy. The time for imagination and new beginnings. The planet and energy are awakening out of hibernation, and nature blooms and grows.

Time to envision and reawaken our dreams, desires, and visions. They are now needed more than ever. We, as a collective shape and change the planet we are living on.

The seeds are ready to sprout, and your projects are ready to unfold and come together if you take one little step after the next.
In Spring the days get longer and longer and more light comes in. It's the transition from the short days with not a lot of light towards the long Summer days full of liveliness, connection, and collaboration time.

Spring is the time for growth, learning, and opening up.

Reflection on how far you have come

How did you take time during the Winter season to integrate and hibernate?

What parts did you reflect on in the last season of introversion?

Where did you get clarity during the Winter season?

What will you anchor in and take with you from the past season?

Where were you at the beginning of the Winter season, at the end of December, and what intentions did you set for yourself?

Where are you now?

Which of the intentions set at the beginning of the year did you reach?

Which of the intentions you set are not relevant anymore, and you can let them go?

Which are still important to you and you will take the next steps towards them?

How will you celebrate your achievements from the last Winter season?

What was your word for the year and how do you feel about it?

I have a *grateful* heart for

Vision on where you want to go

Which seeds did you plant and are now ready to sprout?

What is the most important project you will focus on this Spring?

How will you nurture and take care of your intentions so they can grow?

How much space will you give to them?

Where do you want to commit?

What do you want to practice?

What do you want to let go?

What do you want to invite more of into your life?

What are the three most important intentions you set at the beginning of the year? What about them changed?

1.

On a scale from 1 to 10 how willing are you to invest yourself in making them a reality?

I hope it happens	I am willing to invest myself	I will do whatever it takes

2.

On a scale from 1 to 10 how willing are you to invest yourself in making them a reality?

I hope it happens	I am willing to invest myself	I will do whatever it takes

3.

On a scale from 1 to 10 how willing are you to invest yourself in making them a reality?

I hope it happens	I am willing to invest myself	I will do whatever it takes

What changed? What needs to go? What do you want to invite into your life and business?

Which one is the most important to you and a priority this season? Usually the one with the highest rating.

Lead yourself
from the inside out

Is there an area you need support or accountability?

What new things do you want to learn?

In which way did you expand your comfort zone in the last season?

How will you grow and expand your current comfort zone? Share three things that feel outside your comfort zone that would make you grow if you would do them.

1.

2.

3.

To what actions do you regularly commit? What do you want to practice?

In which way will you hold yourself accountable?

Map out the steps you need to take to get from where you are today, to where you want to be at the beginning of Summer!

WHERE I AM TODAY

WHERE I WANT TO BE

Trust your *journey*

Drop into the vision of your ideal day. How does your ideal day look and feel like? Write it down from morning to evening.

You find a guided meditation on thesoulofbusinesscircle.com

Anchor in your vision and intention

Reflect on your word for the year.

Allow yourself to feel. What did the word teach you? What does still feel right? What changed about your word?

Create a vision board for Spring.

Collect images that feel right for you and cut or print them out. Your soul knows what you desire to let yourself be guided and choose the images that speak to you at the moment without analyzing them.

Your vision board:

Your liberation and freedom serve the world.
Your love and healing serve the collective and our planet.
Your energy mastery creates your reality.

Building the best life for ourselves we can imagine and live in alignment with our soul and core values is not selfish. This is not saying that privilege doesn't exist. It does and for many, it is really real. The chaos in the world can break open places inside of us and in the collective that were neatly hidden before.

Energy doesn't lie.
Hiding back the things that broke out and became clear and visible is not solving the root cause of the problem which to me is the disconnection to our hearts, our lack of self-trust, and to come together beyond the division we see on the surface level.

I know we humans have shared dreams of unity, peace, healing, and love.

Doing your work and creating the most beautiful life and business you are capable of imagining you don't take away from others but inspire others and support others to see what is possible. For you and them.

Leading by example.
Leading with embodiment and grounded truth.

The life you build and create and where you invest your energy is the legacy you leave behind beyond your current physical embodiment of flesh.

How do you want to move, influence, and co-create this place here on earth?

Confidence and Clarity

Summer is the energy of water. The perfect time to trust, lean into the flow of life, and enjoy the outward energy through connections and collaborations.

The season of Summer starts with the longest day of the year, and from there the days will get shorter and energy is decreasing heading towards Autumn where the day with an equal length of the day and night marks the start.

Now is the time of the year where nature is fully alive and vibrant. Live happens outside, and the days are long and full of adventure and connection. After we climbed up through Springtime and sprouted, we now can stretch our leaves. Our connection with source energy, to our essence, and inner guidance comes easily.

Let's open our hearts, carry our ideas into the world, share inspiration and soulfully connect with the world around us.

Reflection on how far you have come

Where are you right now in your life?

Where are you right now in your business?

How do you feel about this?

Where were you at the beginning of Spring?

What was your intention for this past season of Spring?

What has changed for you? How has it changed?

What did you learn and want to remember for the future?

Which of your intentions did manifest and become reality?

What didn't manifest and why?

What do you want to let go?

Where do you need to readjust and change?

Where do you need to forgive and make space for flow and ease?

What are the negative consequences if you let go, release, and forgive?

Is your freedom worth the risk?

Releasing ritual

Releasing what holds us back supports us in making space for what we desire and want to call into our lives.

Summer is a perfect time, as this is the peak of high and outward energy and from here on the days start to get shorter again and the energy moves back inwards, which helps you with leaning into the flow and letting go of what doesn't serve you anymore.

- Connect with a challenge or question you may have
- Center yourself in your heart and close your eyes
- Feel if and where in your body you feel any discomfort
- Locate this discomfort feel how this discomfort feels like
- Make a conscious decision in your mind that you let go of it and free yourself
- Feel into the discomfort and visualize how this discomfort starts to soften and dissolve
- Feel the lightness of your shoulders and how your heart opens up
- Take some time to rest, journal, or do whatever feels good to you at the moment

Do this as many times as you need. It may soften and make you flow only a little bit the first time, or it will dissolve and release all the tension from one second to the other. There is no right or wrong with this. Do what feels good and feels aligned with you.

I have a
grateful
heart for

What do you celebrate?

How will you celebrate?

What was your word for the year? How do you feel about it now?

Vision on where you want to go

How do you want to feel during Summer?

When do you feel this way?

How can you invite more of these feelings into your life?

What will be different if you invite more of these feelings into your life?

How do you show up in your day-to-day life if you become the person you desire to be?

What do you want to do more of?

What do you want to do less of?

Lean into the
flow of life

How will you grow and expand your current comfort zone? Share three things that feel outside your comfort zone that would make you grow if you would do them.

1.

2.

3.

To what actions do you invite into your life?

What fears or worries hold you back from trusting?

Your highest *timeline*

If you imagine the highest timeline of your life and business. Who would you be? What would you have? What would you do?

Where and in which way do you need to trust yourself?

Where and in which way do you need to trust in being guided in your life?

How could you collaborate and create new connections?

What are the three most important intentions you set at the beginning of the year? What about them changed?

1.

On a scale from 1 to 10 how willing are you to invest yourself in making them a reality?

I hope it happens	I am willing to invest myself	I will do whatever it takes

2.

On a scale from 1 to 10 how willing are you to invest yourself in making them a reality?

I hope it happens	I am willing to invest myself	I will do whatever it takes

3.

On a scale from 1 to 10 how willing are you to invest yourself in making them a reality?

I hope it happens	I am willing to invest myself	I will do whatever it takes

What changed? Where can you lean in more and trust?

Which one is the most important to you and a priority this season? Usually the one with the highest rating.

Connect to the guidance of your heart

Anchor in your vision and intention

Reflect on your word for the year.

Allow yourself to feel. What did the word teach you? What does still feel right? What did change about your word?

Create a vision board for Summer.

Collect images that feel right for you and cut or print them out. Your soul knows what you desire. Let yourself be guided, and choose the images that speak to you at the moment without analyzing them.

Your vision board:

Leadership to me is following our inner compass and aligning to our soul and the truth that we came to believe in based on our own experience.

Pure truth leads to clear and confident action.
Pure truth to me is a balance of rational decisions from our heads and deep trust in our hearts.

The layer of fear that weaves and intertwines between you and your full sovereignty needs to be unraveled to get to the depth of who you are.

These layers of fear are what keeps us collectively stuck in the matrix of scarcity and not-enoughness.

Peeling back layer after layer of conditioning. Looking beyond the shadow where there is light again.

There is a version for every one of us who is, was, and always will be whole.

There is a version of our beautiful planet earth that is in balance, unity, love, abundance, and peace.

Our energy is what weaves and co-creates the tapestry of this world. This is our responsibility. The responsibility from each one of us. This is our power.

We can consciously drop into the embodiment of our inner essence and share from this place with the world, or we can let our energy sicker away into all the things that distract us and keep us stuck in the old paradigm of scarcity. The news, the television, the distractions, the scrolling on social media, the alcohol, the excuses dims our power from the outside in, but there is another way.

We can first access our inner truth and cycle and build the energy from there until it overflows into the world and we become the influence instead of being influenced.

We are the freedom keepers. We are the visionaries that build the world from the inside out.

Harvest your Desires

Autumn is earth energy. Grounding and rooting. It's the time of the year when the fruits are ready to be harvested and your manifestation from the beginning of the year are ready to be fulfilled and taken from in the physical realm.

Take some time to connect with your inner guidance, your core desires, and shaping a clear vision for your desired future lifestyle is an ongoing practice, not a one-time task on your to-do list.
Making space for what you want and letting go of everything that doesn't serve you anymore starts within you and from there manifests into your reality.

Taking regular time to connect with your desires and to give your soul space, will help you to hear your inner voice clear and prepare you to make confident and aligned actions on your own and unique path.

Reflection on how far you have come

How did you take time during the Summer season to go with the flow?

What about you do you like?

What are some accomplishments and celebrations of your life you are proud of?

What are your gifts and talents that support you on your path?

What are your three biggest desires for your life and business?

Anchor in your vision and intention

Reflect on your word for the year.

Allow yourself to feel. What did the word teach you? What does still feel right? What did change about your word?

How did this word guide you? What are the things you can harvest thanks to this word?

What abundance did you attract into your life this year?

Who have you become?

What are the three most important intentions you set at the beginning of the year? What did they bring in your life?

1.

On a scale from 1 to 10 how much growth and abundance did this intention gift you?

I did let it go and it changed	It brougth some change in my life and business	It invited a lot of expansion and abundace

2.

On a scale from 1 to 10 how much growth and abundance did this intention gift you?

I did let it go and it changed	It brougth some change in my life and business	It invited a lot of expansion and abundace

3.

On a scale from 1 to 10 how much growth and abundance did this intention gift you?

I did let it go and it changed	It brougth some change in my life and business	It invited a lot of expansion and abundace

What are your biggest learnings that you want to anchor in?

Which one do you want to deepen and connect with during this coming season of Autumn? In which way can you lean in more and build on what is already there?

Investing in yourself is essential

How much closer did you move towards those intentions?

What is still between you and them?

Where did you get support for yourself?

What were your biggest challenges in this period?

What supported you and how did you deal with those challenges through these periods?

How did these challenges help you to get where you are today? If you are still working through a particular challenge, what would you desire as the perfect outcome?

I have a *grateful* heart for

What is the highest vision you hold for your life in your future?

What are you ready to receive and allow into your life now?

What do you need to let go of?

In which areas do you need support to reach your vision?

What do you need to commit to?

Where do you need to take responsibility?

Map out the steps that you need to take to get from where you are today, to where you want to be at the end of Autumn!

WHERE I AM TODAY

WHERE I WANT TO BE

How do you want to feel on this journey?

How will you grow and expand your current comfort zone? Share three things that feel outside your comfort zone that would make you grow if you would do them.

1.

2.

3.

To what actions do you invite into your life?

What fears or worries hold you back from trusting?

Harvest your accomplishments

What are some things in your life you started that need finishing and wrapping up? Write a list with five things that need closing.

Anchor in your vision and intention

Reflect on your word for the year.

Allow yourself to feel. What did the word teach you? What does still feel right? What did change about your word?

Create a vision board for Autumn.

Collect images that feel right for you and cut or print them out. Your soul knows what you desire. Let yourself be guided and choose the images that speak to you at the moment without analyzing them.

Your vision board:

Start from where you are and with what you have, you are ready. Own your essence and allow your light to illuminate the world around you and your love to touch the hearts of those who need it.

Building a life and business that are deeply aligned with your essence is a way of serving the whole.

If you integrate your love and share it the energy you are filled up with emanates from you out into the world.

Your alignment is your energy signature and your energy signature is your inner vibration and how you feel.
This inner vibration, ripples into the world, just the same way as the ripples from a stone you let fall into the water or the waves that move through the ocean, your energy waves move through the world.

Your brand is a way for you to amplify this energy signature of yours. A soulful business is a catalyst to create change and healing to create a world on our beautiful planet earth that is more equal, filled with love, and where we truly all can do the things we are good in and that fills us up.

Our work, when we are in alignment and are doing what we came here to do, fills us up with energy.

Work that depletes us, is work that is out of alignment.

THERE IS
NO BETTER
TIME TO
LEAD
YOURSELF
THAN NOW

Soulful business
inspiration

If you liked this journal and want to dive in deeper on your soulful business journey you find gifts and inspiration on this link:

thesoulofbusinesscircle.com

My intention for you is that you truly believe that you can do business from the inside out and that you become your own most trusted mentor. Trust this journey of yours of growing your soul project and supporting the world with your light.

Everything you need to know is already inside of you.

Thank you,

I am deeply grateful for everything that went into this book.

Without the help and support of others, I wouldn't be the person I am today, and I wouldn't have been able to write this book.

My heartfelt thank you to every one of my clients who inspire me daily. Sincere gratitude to my daughter Li Tara Koch for making the photographs in this book.

I am deeply grateful for the support and inspiration from my husband, both of my daughters, my grandfather, and all loved ones I have in my life.

Thank you for filling this journal out, your energy creates change in the world.
I am deeply grateful you are here.

With Love,
Eos

www.ingramcontent.com/pod-product-compliance
Ingram Content Group UK Ltd.
Pitfield, Milton Keynes, MK11 3LW, UK
UKHW060125010826
14089UKWH00006B/156

9 788409 342617